THE QUEST FOR SALINITY

A JOURNEY FROM FRESH TO SALTWATER FLY FISHING

CAPTAIN DENNY SEABRIGHT

<u>Dedication</u>

To my brother that passed

My brother that will

My wife I love

My Sons

The Granddaughters

And the Dogs

Table of Contents

Our Beginnings

1

I flung the fly back and forth over the river as I had seen in the magazines waiting for a bass to leap in the air and inhale my offering. My twelve-year-old imagination had already caught it, cleaned it, and put it in my pan.

Growing tired and a little bored I retreated back to the old Inn my parents rented an apartment in for the summers.

The old Capon Inn sat on the bank of the Capon River in West Virginia and from the sign along the hard cap it was once a grand vacation destination for presidents and wealthy travelers.

It was where while rummaging through one of many junk closets I came across the old bamboo fly rod. It had a broken tip that I bent a piece of wire and replaced with black tape my father fixed everything with.

I had drawers full of Outdoor Life, Sports Afield and Playboy magazines to study so I paid a little more attention to the article the second time around, noticing an important step I had left out. The fisherman was to stop flinging and let the fly settle on the water like the little fella was tired.

At that point as it drifted overhead in the current, the fly would be attacked resulting in it being hooked, and it was game on! I tripped running down the steps in my haste to get back on the river which by now laid calm with longer shadows and pesky little white bugs filling the air.

I cast the heavy line attached to this white beat up piece of feather maybe ten feet out in the river and about fell over myself when all hell broke loose. A two-pound smallmouth erupted out of the water with my feather in its jaw.

The fight was short as I hadn't got far enough in the article to realize you were supposed to let the line slide through your fingers, an action that would result in hundreds of burns over the next five decades. I sat there in shock reenacting the event that just unfolded smiling, realizing that now, I was a fly fisherman.

By the end of the summer when our weekends at Capon came to an end my after-school time would be spent divided between mowing the grass and chasing bluegills at a nearby farm pond.

I carried that long rod while my dad still used a Zebco 303 with ten-pound test for everything from bass to panfish. It annoyed me to hear that heavy bobber and weight hit the water as I was now a fly fisherman.

He, as most fly fishermen grew very fast in his talent and dreams since our blood is of the type A or B.

Most live in their own world not really caring about what others think.

The first chapter was the first step in a fly fisher's life. That being finding out about the activity and its fundamentals.

This is where most figure it's too hard or not worth the extra effort and fall back to the normal spinning rod.

Trout and Skittles

2

My casts were getting better and I even learned the roll cast so I could fish a stocked trout stream on weekends.

My first trout sent me over the edge. On the first day of the season my dad dropped me off at eleven o'clock so I could get my place beside the bankers, brick masons and doctors that lined the bank on the first Saturday in April.

Most used worms, salmon eggs or Velveeta cheese they rolled into balls and froze the night before.

The awaited noon hour struck, and the peaceful creek sounded like it was ground zero in a hailstorm. The water was a froth from the barrage of lures and cheese baits. I froze for a moment taking in all the back slapping, whooping and hollering, slipping and sliding, and the fish massacre taking place in my once quiet pool.

Snapping out of it I sent a roll cast flying only to have my Woolly Bugger lodge in an oak branch behind me. That was the first of many moments of frustrations I would experience being a fly fisherman. As I crawled up the muddy bank to save my fly, I overheard some snickering and laughing from the bobber brigade below me, who by now were almost limited out with trout laying at their feet on chain and rope stringers soon to be cleaned for dinner.

I recovered my fly and worked my way down the creek to take the place of Mr. Brooks, a local car salesman that had his four trout and was leaving.

"They're in here son, tell your dad hey" as he limped up the bank. I had this hole all to myself now and I felt like I just stepped off a floatplane in Alaska.

Screw the roll cast I thought to myself as I had an opening behind me in the trees, so I just cast, landing my black bugger in the lee of a tree stump. I wiggled my rod tip with the black tape now starting to fray and noticed a swirl under the water, "A trout!"I pulled my line in a motion I later learned was a strip and worked the jumping, spinning maniac fish to the gravel bar where I pulled my prize out of the water.

There were no cell phones with cameras in those days so the only proof of that twelve-inch rainbow at my feet is etched in my mind more than six decades later.

I slipped the trout in my hand-me-down moss lined creel. I was now a fly fisherman.

Fly fishing originally came about as a way of delivering a light bait, in this case a hand tied imitation of a flying insect.

Due to the weight of the offering it would be impossible to cast it any distance without using a heavy weight that certainly would scare the fish when it hit the water.

Trout were the quarry intended to pursue as their diet consisted mostly of floating insects that sometimes were so small you could barely see them with the naked eye.

The fly line is made with a heavy slippery outer part to slide through the guides and your fingers. This line uses its own weight to deliver the fly but must be cast by loading the rod in a back and forth rhythm.

That rhythm is the action that takes practice and practice takes time that most find hard to come by.

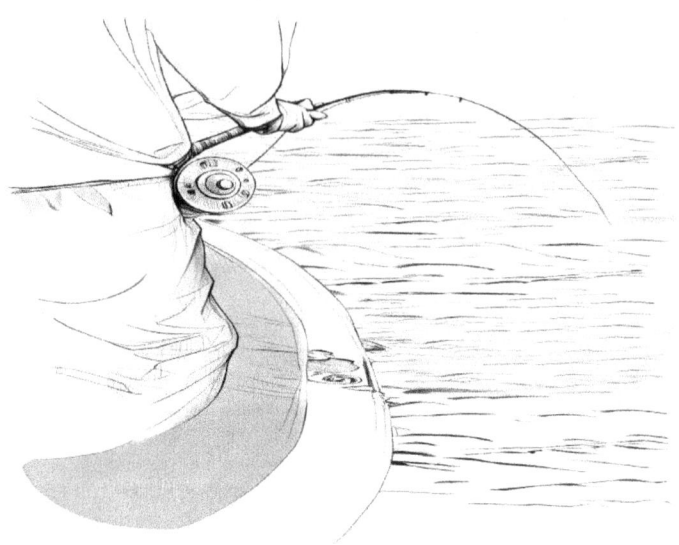

<u>On the Reel</u>

<u>3</u>

Plop, plop, plop, ka-plop! The largemouth sucked the popper off the surface leaving a hole the size of a drywall bucket.

This tug on my stripping hand got to be like a drug forcing me to skip school, be late for dinner and lights out. Those damn American Sportsmen shows in my formative years were as bad as the Playboy magazine's up at Capon that I now paid a bit more attention to.

13

I had to split my addictions between pretty girls and the river. A tough one but --I was a fly fisherman.

That old taped up bamboo that I wish I had today was replaced by a mail order fiberglass rig with a Martin reel. The reel had a knob on the side when turned would slow the fish. Laugh out loud, they would say these days. Where the hell am I going to find a fish of that caliber.

I dreamed of a fish that "would put me on the reel", a fish so fast or powerful that the line would burn your fingers to the bone or worse, break the rod.

The plan calls for you to milk the line left over from the cast through your hand until the drag takes over and slows the fish.

Most freshwater fish are too small or slow for this plan.

I saw a tv show about fly fishing for carp with flies that resembled a mulberry that had fallen in the water. We had them in the Shenandoah River, where I had been spending more time chasing smallmouth bass these days. This was way before Muskies had been introduced to the river.

I'd seen carp as big as logs while floating and started my plan of action. By this time, I had a cheap vice to tie flies, so I built a blueprint. A fly made of twisted pieces of yarn spun around a hook that had soldering wire wrapped around it for weight. The yarn was from purple stock of my grandmother's, that she had laid back for a sweater, but hey it was just a small piece. The finished fly looked more like something in a Tom and Jerry cartoon but I was ready to fling it.

Off to the river I went in my hand me down aluminum canoe that my older brothers had used to recreate a scene off of Deliverance and wrapped around a tree. It was a little rough, but it floated.

As I came to the deep section of the river where I had seen them laid up on previous trips there was a mulberry tree hanging over the river with a group of large carp hanging out waiting for a berry to drop. I set my homemade brick anchor and observed, a thing fly fishermen do.

A berry dropped with a plop and two medium carp swam to intercept. This is a good thing because when there are more than one, competition sets in and it's easier to fool them into thinking your offering is the real deal. Some say curiosity killed the cat, but I say greed did the deed myself.

After they went back to loafing and calmed down I made my cast. The make believe berry fell with a loud thud and was accepted as being real and the two swam over with the fatty being beat out by the smaller fish as usually happens. The fish was smaller but still at least fifteen pounds more than enough to make my 7# weight buck and strain. The old Martin reel did its job letting line out slowly with resistance like it was intended to.

The fight was long enough, and it had taken place on the reel so there, I was a saltwater fly fisherman in training.

The act of being "on the reel" is one that is sought after by half of the modern fly fisher's out there, the other half are content with catching smaller fish that they can merely pull in with their hands in a stripping motion.

Captain Denny is in the first half and longed to connect with a worthy fish powerful enough to overwhelm the rod and line on its own, longing to have the fish pull so hard that it forced the angler to give in and let the drag on the reel do the work.

The addiction to it led to the quest for bigger fish that lived in salt water.

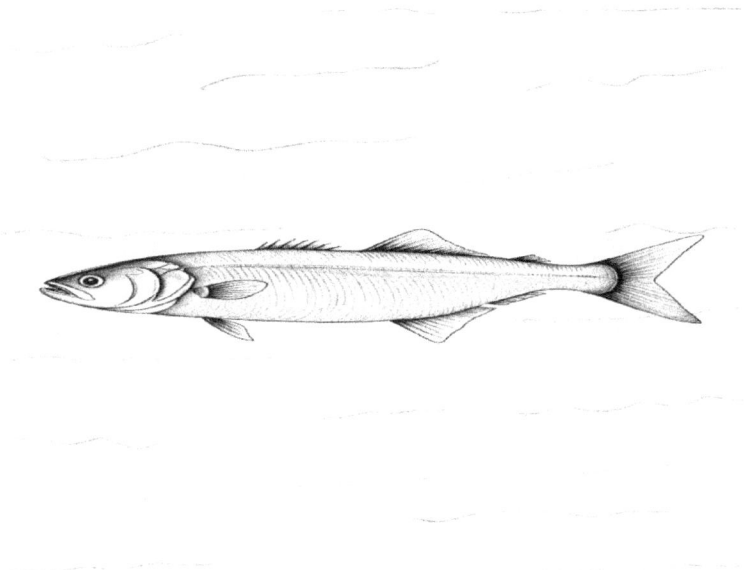

Feel the Burn

4

I was invited on a trip to the Chesapeake Bay by a co-worker in pursuit of bluefish and jumped at the chance. They were catching chopper blues on trolling gear which I wasn't thrilled about but asked if I could bring my long rod since I was a fly fisherman.

They laughed and said shuur, and laughed some more. These were the real variety weighing up to 18 pounds, not the Taylor blues that came after the early '80s.

18

They told me of the blues chasing bunker to the surface and busting in a commotion that made you hold your ears. The boat was stopped and at that point huge poppers were thrown with spinning rods into the froth for lack of a better word. My imagination ran wild hearing that as I had poppers. I caught bass on them in my farm pond.

I couldn't understand why while discussing my strategy the crew would burst out laughing, but I brushed it off as just beer talk.

The weekend came and we headed southeast out of the mountains to the Virginia Beach area of the bay. Pulling that ole twenty foot cuddy cabin with a Dodge Charger, bumper dragging the ground with my trusty 7 weight by my side soon to be outmatched.

We had just gotten to the foothills when all agreed it was a nice place to piss beer. Unfortunately, a jar head Virginia State Trooper thought otherwise as he came up from behind shouting that Virginia had bathrooms and some other unpleasant remarks.

It then occurred to me my buddy's car had West Virginia plates as I walked around the car. You had to laugh.

After our verbal ass whooping, we were free to go with the next stop being Foxy Lady and motel, not necessarily in that order.

Foxy Lady was a tittie bar the boys were fond of apparently as when we went through the door a healthy specimen greeted them by name and a hug. Game on.

Eight AM came early with our heads the size of Texas but we got through and with tires sliding down the ramp managed to get the heavy boat in the water.

This was my first encounter with any saltwater fish and would not only burn my hand but also the memory into my brain for the ruination of my soul.

We made the ten-mile run to the spot and put out the trolling rods. Fortunately for us we saw ahead what looked like a waterspout I had seen only in pictures. The water boiled in an area the size of a football field.

Scrambling to get the trolling tackle in while getting the massive spinning rods out was frenzied to say the least.

We approached the school and like the descriptions, the noise was deafening.

Menhaden were thrown in the air, blood and scales covered the water and huge poppers were cast into the melee.

'Fish on!" Mark yelled and screamed in delight as the line ripped from the reel. The other boy likewise hooked up immediately after.

They went to the front of the boat allowing me to make a few false casts and land my fly at the edge of the school.

My popper disappeared and line screamed through my fingers causing severe pain and I let go. The line wrapped around the reel handle and "Snap"! My leader broke and my fish was gone with one of the two bugs I had brought.

The fish went down, and the boys got one of the two they had hooked. As it lay on the deck, I couldn't get over the size of this fish: it was mean looking with teeth like a dog flopping around throwing blood all over the place making the boat look like a Civil War hospital. Insane, just insane.

I had to reflect over this. My pain came back and looking down at my bleeding hand, broken leader and well--- I just shook.

I didn't know if it was from adrenaline, pain or fear, but I shook.

We looked around and far off in the distance we saw either another school or the same one that resurfaced but fish were breaking and we were running, running and gunning they call it on the bay, an exciting way to fish for sure.

I tied on another leader and my last popper and was ready when we stopped upwind so I could cast: my boys wanted to see this. I flung the popper into the target zone and like before it was instant hook up, wheels up, game on or whatever your favorite slang is. The line came tight to the reel, textbook, rod at 45 degrees; let's go! And so, we did; I watched as my hundred dollar fly line disappeared into the backing and smoke came from that old Martin reel. I felt helpless as my freshwater rig self-destructed before my eyes.

I was now a saltwater fly fisherman in ruins as the last of my backing went to the arbor knot which, like I did, gave up.

The captain and author got a taste of a saltwater fish in this story, burning not only his fingers but a memory into his brain for the rest of his life.

The power and grit of this fish put him on a change of course that would take him to far away places and some not so distant.

Saltwater fish are accessible to a large part of the angling population even being found in harbors in or near our largest cities across the globe.

One does not have to board a plane and travel to distant locations to fish for them, but it is a large part of the equation.

As his fishing buddy always said, "getting there is half the fun."

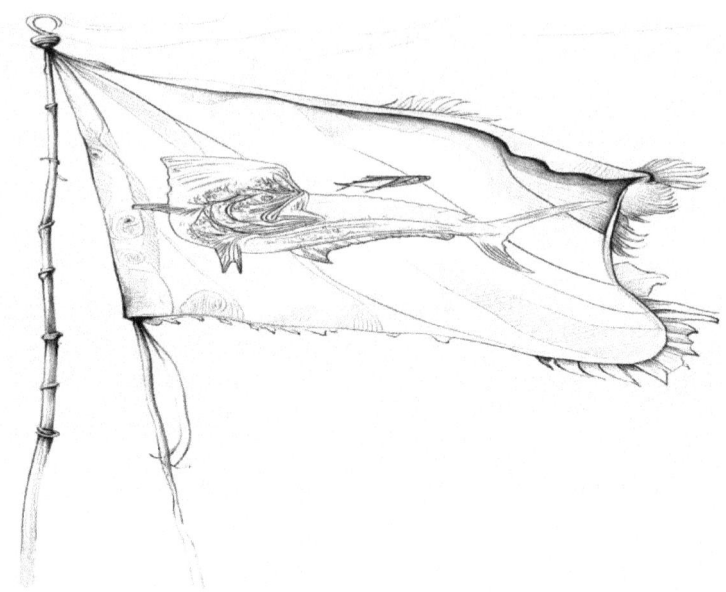

<u>The Danger Zone</u>

<u>5</u>

As the saying goes, the two happiest days are when you buy a boat and when you sell one; this was happy day #1.

I bought a boat capable of running offshore, a 21' Trophy with twin two stroke mosquito sprayers on the back.

I named her Danger Zone to match her mission. She got me offshore to catch marlin and mahi-mahi, and bluefish and stripers in the Chesapeake.

On a trip off of the dreaded Oregon inlet we ran 32 miles to the Point, a canyon so to speak where baitfish got slammed against the jog in the Continental Shelf with the current. After screwing holes in the ocean trolling for an empty morning we saw some free jumping Mahi in the distance. They were chicken Dolphin so not big enough to be called Mahi-Mahi, just Mahi. Laugh out loud.

They were surrounding an old duck blind that had been washed out to sea, hundreds of them. My mate filled the cooler with a big 750 Penn spinning rod but I saw an opportunity to catch a saltwater fish on my fly rod because I was a fly fisherman.

I crawled up on the bow and made a cast. The green fish exploded from below blowing my fly out of the water but when it landed two more pounced on it.

I cast and played with them for hours almost forgetting how far we were from home. The water was so calm it was one of those days when you look out and the sky and the water combine on the horizon and you think you are in a wonderland, a wonderland full of hungry fish. Pinch me, was this a dream?

October brought unsafe cold fronts to the ocean side so I would relocate DZ to the bayside to target striped bass as they fed, fattening up for the winter.

Every fall they gorge themselves on bunker coming out of the rivers and light tackle fishermen hunt them in the run and gun method.

It can be an unreal day with fish to 20 pounds smashing your Clouser Minnow or Sand Eel imitations.

Using a sinking line, we dredged the depths for the larger ones but to me the ones on the surface crashing top water flies were way more fun.

The Danger Zone had a good ten year run but happy day #2 came and we parted ways.

Looking back to the time when captain Denny was compounding his sea time and learning the saltwater game, this chapter gives some insight to the lifestyle of a boat owner.

A lot of people feel that owning a boat is not worth the headache or cost associated with it. They get tired of the seemingly constant breakdowns and bad weather days, the friends that love to ride but forgot their wallet.

Sometimes the right thing to do as in this case is to downsize, other times it makes more sense to travel to different locations if that suits the angler's lifestyle.

Congo Air

6

Without a boat what's a man to do, Well Willis let's get a plane.

Hey, if Flip and Jose can travel the world, so can I.

I got my shirt cut on a spring morning when my instructor said "stop the plane" on our way back to the tarmac after some practice flights. He got out in the grass and said: "take 'er around a few times and call it".

What the hell, I thought, this isn't what I had envisioned, just up and get out! I guess he thought I wouldn't get nervous, but he was wrong.

After all the dust settled, I had my sights set on bonefish in the Bahamas. Flying into an old remote airstrip like a Zane Grey "wanna be" was in the cards so let me tell you about my first bone.

I had a friend that fished with me, let's call him Joe. He would drop what he was doing and go at the drop of a hat. Joe had a cute girlfriend, so plans were made. The two couples would fly a beat up old Cessna Sky wagon to the Bahamas and go fishing.

My flight instructor took a liking to me because of my go or blow attitude so he agreed to buy the added insurance waiver for the out of country trip and made a bet with me that he would never see me again.

A new pilot flying to an offshore destination with limited navigation aids was a risky business back then, but plans were made and I found a rental house on Long Island 350 miles offshore of Miami.

Upon getting to Fort Pierce where we were to rent our life raft and depart from, a young lineman noticed at the last moment that our plane had N numbers that were the old 3" version and informed us that without 12" numbers we could leave but we would not be permitted to land back in the good ole USA. Well I had a liking for Apple pie and hot pants, so we came up with a plan and saved the day with a four dollar roll of duct tape.

Yep, we looked like we belonged in Alaska, not on the tarmac of a Florida airport.

We departed the next morning on a bluebird morning with light winds, hold that thought. Flying an ADF bearing which is nothing more than tracking an AM radio station in Nassau on a needle. We got about half way there and I was seriously beginning to doubt there was a Bahamas after all we were dead smack in the Bermuda Triangle. But the dark blue ocean turned turquoise and I started to breathe again.

I flew lower and followed the chains of islands on my chart across my lap to Deadman's Cay airport, a dirt strip in the middle of nowhere.

We were on a long final for runway 27 in a 20-knot crosswind when I pulled the carburetor heat knob and it came out in my hand. My hand yes came out in my hand. No one is laughing out loud now.

Carb heat is needed in humid conditions to keep the carburetor from freezing up when power is reduced for landing and immediately, she started missing and bucking. I was committed at this point, low on fuel and no bigger airport close.

Joe was frantically trying to stuff the cable back in the panel before the babbling babes in the back noticed but too late. "Is that supposed to do that?" she asked. But I was too busy to respond. I had but one chance to stick this flying truck to the postage stamp size airstrip below.

I'm writing this with a neat Scotch and dribble of sweat running down my neck at that memory, so it must have worked out.

We had an incredible stay, met some nice natives and yes, I caught my first bonefish.

This was the last trip for my ole Martin Fly Reel and glass rod from Cabela's. I figured it almost landed a 15-pound Bluefish so a much smaller bone would be noooooo problem, right?

The island had no bonefish camps or guide outfits with spiffy shirts and flats skiffs, this was before all that on Long Island.

I found a young man named Deric at the bar that had a small boat and a big stick that claimed he knew where they lived, the bones that is.

"Right ova theya," he said while pointing into the sun as a school came down the Mangrove shoreline. I finally made them out and cast only to place my line over them and scatter the bunch like I had the Covid.

We continued for the morning with Deric calling out fish as he would say, "Shock" sticking his pole in the sides of lemon sharks that got too close. You could tell there was no love for shocks, no love.

As the sun got high and I could make them out better a pair came toward us and I caught the flash in the distance. Without saying a word I flung on'em.

Man was I a fly fisherman now, I thought, then this pissy ass 2-pound fish commenced to whip my ass.

I was into the backing before I could say "fish on". Deric was as surprised as I that I finally connected. Finally, after gaining and loosing line several times it submitted to the guide's gentle touch. Holding him upside down to calm him Deric removed the fly and handed him to me.

I swear it was not unlike when the nurse handed me my newborn son for the first time. The looks on the guy's faces as they looked into my eyes, surely was a moment I will never forget for as long as I live. There were more caught on that trip, even Joe caught one in a mud where they had been kicking up sand, feeding. He got to feel the burn, so all was good.

We had some close calls with storms on the way back to the mountains and were a few days late when we pulled up in front of my instructor's office trailing grey tape twenty feet behind the plane. But him smiling and shaking his head was evidence that he'd forgotten the bet.

Flying solo, emergency landings and worse weather days make for an exciting angling adventure, as felt here in this story of travel, first fish and happy people.

The Bahamas has a special place in the author's heart as you will come to find out in the following chapters.

A blood type that can make one do extraordinary things had to be the determining factor in making a young carpenter spend all his hard-earned spare money on flying lessons with dreams of faraway destinations only accessible by small plane.

A *go or blow* attitude and friends and family that were very trustworthy helped create the storyline of Congo Air.

Air travel back then in the islands was a little different as navigation aids were only available when you were at a higher altitude and able to connect to Nassau or the United States mainland.

The story was just one of many that took place on that trip and others in the quest to find fish in remote places.

Tallahassee Red

7

Traveling to fishing destinations seemed to be the new norm and a trip to Apalachicola Florida was laid out to try to catch a baby tarpon. Why my buds chose this place is beyond me other than the famous oysters but the first class plane tickets were free from my friend's brother so I thought: hell, lets go!

We were to stay in town for a few days and fish with a young hotshot guide that told me I had a weasel mentality like him. I didn't know how to take that, but we soon launched looking for tarpon, redfish or trout.

The weather was surly, so we ended up splitting up with my bud going pan fishing with another guide and me and the bro going tarpon fishing.

What we ended up catching was lady fish, they've been called the poor man's tarpon because they look just like one, have the same mental problem and are easy and cheap to catch.

Any port in a storm I always say, and we enjoyed the crazy fish on my new Islander fly reel. What a difference, it was attached to an Orvis 8 wt with a real saltwater butt. I was fishing in high seas now baby, a real saltwater fly fisherman.

Back at the hotel swapping stories we got thirsty and a place called the Oasis was at the end of the street.

The saloon had swinging doors like in western movies and when I swung them open with friend's brother in tow, well there was no going back.

No matter how bad a place looks upon entry, when you bust through swinging saloon doors like John Wayne, you can't check the menu, say I'm sorry and slither on out, you just can't.

There were several part Cajun part black characters that looked like they knew the warden by name, a couple bar flies, some more good black folk and a bartender that knew "beer, whiskey and could make change for the pool table" that sat in the middle of the floor being used by some good ole boys at the time.

I ordered some beers and change, sashayed over, put a quarter on the rail and took a seat with bro.

Well come to find out bro had led a sheltered life and was full of questions about the quarter act, had never heard how you can take the table from the previous loser.

He sat there with a Pee Wee Herman look while listening and said, "cool bean" whatever the hell that meant.

My time came as snaggle tooth lost to Mr. Tee and it was game time. The two beers had set in just right and well it was just one of those rare times when it all falls together. In the meantime I caught quarters being laid down out the corner of my eye as these jail birds wanted a piece of me.

We had arrived at this fine establishment just after noon and it was getting dark out. My friend came in to check on us and being sober and well versed on the bar scene tried to evict us but brother was enjoying the show and I was the act, so friend stormed out the doors.

One by one they came after me and one by one they fell. There were no fights or cussing just friendly jabs. I was staying in that happy place two or three beers put you in only because I was too busy to get drunk.

Some talked about Tallahassee Red like they wished it was here, some wished not. Wondering what the hell a Tallahassee Red was, I just figured it was a drink or something as I continued my streak.

Ten O'clock-ish with no dinner came and went, bro kept me in whiskey and beer, so I didn't leave my post but soon I had to piss.

After winning one, I told them I would be right back and when I returned it was there, all there.

No mistaking what a Tallahassee Red was now.

Standing before me opening his leather pool stick case was the biggest, blackest brother with flame red hair and nose rings, I had ever seen.

He inserted his quarter with a grin full of gold and said "Bust em!"

I'm no pool shark; it was just a good night mind ya but it was a good night. I all but run the table leaving my new friend just one chance but no cigar.

Finishing him off, he slammed his stick down on the table and stormed out the door. Brother came up as I was chalking my stick and said, "did he leave?" I said "Naaa, he'll be back," and he did return. He came through the door, grabbed my hand with a couple twisty moves and said, "Good game mon."

About three weeks later my son and I were pulling into the driveway and he said, "What's that?" and I replied, "I don't know" referring to the huge box on the porch.

Not knowing what was in it I cut it open to find an old lobster pot. It took a minute to sink in but I had bought it from a vendor down there to build an end table that still sits here by my couch today.

What they say about brain cells is Vewwy, Vewwy, Twuu.

Wow, at 68 years of age sitting here at the laptop wishing he had it all to do over. What would he change?

Except for a few one nighter's in the "pokey" and some disrespectful times to his wife he probably wouldn't change a thing.

I don't think men like the cap't are made to fit in, they are wanderers full of curiosity, doers of deeds that need to be done.

Unfortunately, the lifestyle can wreak havoc on family life and having a loving spouse that understands is the key. There were times when he had enough of the norm and would take off on trips to anywhere or nowhere for that matter. The reality is the dedication in this book should have been in but one person's name, his loving wife, Theresa or Tee as the outdoor community knows her.

"Always and 4ever"

Relapse
8

Though the saltwater bug had bitten me hard I still lived in the Shenandoah Valley at the time, and fly fishing had dug into the bone.

The Shenandoah River was going through one of its good phases so after acquiring an aluminum Go-Devil boat with a rock and shoulder eating mud motor I spent a lot of time in the current. I did some freelance guiding using a technique that was mostly used in the saltwater at that point.

I would do a controlled drift with the anchor dropped from my poling platform at likely intervals mostly in the rapids where the big ones lived. The fisherman would fan cast ahead and that would be repeated down the river.

One day my son and I were scouting new water and I was on the platform stopping at likely looking areas I could see from my vantage point.

I saw a nice ledge and dropped the mushroom anchor. As the boat coasted to a stop I grabbed my rod and stood to cast. All that momentum combined with the anchor hooking a boulder set forth a chain of events.

A whole lot of physics came into play and I went hurtling, but luckily, I shoved off the right or starboard side as I would come to know. Landing in about a foot of water breaking my brand new $200 shades but no bones.

I stood up shaking the cold water off and hunting my cap, my son was laughing out loud and I was pissed.

There were great days with clients saying they had never caught so many fish in that river, so the technique worked when you stayed on the platform.

A few good years of that and then the fish kill came to the river, and it was back to 6" bass being the norm. I spent a lot of time with my beloved fly rod chasing anything that would eat a fly. Hell, one night we took it instead of a frog gig. A piece of red cloth on a hook in front of Kermit led to a fight and plate of some of the best eating on the planet. Any port in a storm.

I added a cheap 6 wt to my arsenal for bream and crappie in the lake and they were fun but the salt was calling me home and I went.

The biggest difference in fresh and saltwater fishing is the tide and its constant change.

It can get hectic, trying to maneuver around and not get stuck in the process.

Sometimes it can put a hurried pace to the day that takes some of the enjoyment out of it.

The act of fishing as a form of relaxation can be thrown out the window while chasing tides and running from them.

After becoming a true saltwater fisherman it's nice to take a break occasionally. Stop and smell the roses so to speak and in the previous chapter the author did and still does at times.

A reset so to speak. Catch some bream or land locked bass out of a leaky old john boat.

Captain Denny loves to go to a local lake on a warm sunny day in March and throw small flies for crappie and maybe throw a beer back.

Life is good, don't get caught up in the hustle.

Bonefish Hippie

9

After I sold the Danger Zone it freed up some money normally spent on docks, fuel, upkeep and bait. At least that's the way I justified it to the wife to start traveling to the Bahamas frequently. Since she was a sun worshiper it went smoother than expected.

We would drag the kids and another couple to share the house rental and scour the out islands looking for bonefish.

Grand Bahama, Aklins, Crooked and Andros, we did 'em all. On trips we couldn't find another couple we made short hops to the lesser of two evils, Freeport because Nassau just wasn't the Bahamas.

My youngest son Cody and I fished with one of the Sawyer boys on Green Turtle Cay off Abaco at times.

On a trip there once his reel that he had acquired from a well-known outdoor supply company became a paper weight that still sits on his desk.

Cody was about 14 years old as I recollect and took to casting flies like a pro. We were on a creek at high tide when Sawyer said "12 o'clock, monster bone!"

40 feet ahead and closing was a massive bone that looked like a battleship. He was so wide. Cody made a perfect cast that connected, and all hell broke loose.

That fish decided he wasn't coming into the boat right away, did an about face and fled the scene.

It was one of the shortest fights I have watched, Cody holding the rod up at 45 degrees, the line sliding through the guides to the reel, textbook.

The scene transferred from a back-slapping moment to one of panic as the reel started to smoke. The speed in which that bone escaped was insane, there was nothing any of us could do but to watch as the aluminum spool welded itself to the frame and stop.

The result was a bonefish with a small fly lodged in his mouth as free as Willy and a very hot, soon to be a paper weight.

My wife Tee, and I were fishing the Airport flats with one of the Pinder boys and my wife had to use the potty so we beached at a place with porta Johns we could walk up to.

On return as we walked down to the boat with fritters in hand, there stood Joe with my rod in two pieces. WTF?

"I just cast it once mon!" "No problem bro it must have got nicked in transit." He felt bad about that, but Orvis has a good warranty and I used it.

Good thing he had a spare.

On another trip to that island Joe offered my son Rick and I to come to Mcleans Town on the other end of the island. Seventy miles of road as straight as an arrow with old cars that had broken lining the road in places like some of the airstrips I landed on. The Bahamas was just different then.

This was where Joe and his family lived and was his private honey hole.

It was a calm hot day in August but after a short boat ride we ended up in bonefish heaven. Totally unspoiled real estate.

We stepped out of the boat with Rick joining him, and I heading in the opposite direction. We lost count how many tailing fish we saw and caught that day. It is a memory etched in my mind beside my first forever.

Bin Laden showed his ass one month before a trip with my friend's brother to Grey's Point, Aklins to stalk ghosts in the very shallow water there. The head guide Elvis called me Osama because I wore a head scarf all the time.

One day we were headed to a flat to wade, when we saw a huge sickle tail breaking the surface. "Permit!" At that time the new lodge hadn't landed one yet, and I wanted him bad.

Elvis poled us toward him until it was too shallow and I abandoned ship in pursuit.

It was like one of those out of body experiences where I saw myself through the eyes of my buddies.

I slowly stalked doing the stingray shuffle toward the king of the flats, he was coming my way closing the gap 60, 50, 40, then 30 feet. I cast, landing my crab pattern perfectly in front and stripped. Closer he swam, following until my leader was just outside the rod tip. Just nine feet and the last thing I remember was looking at a set of lips Pamela Anderson would be proud to sport.

With a boil he spun and was out of my life, my guide's life, and the lodge's life.

We flew into Congo Town on the big Island of Andros in search of the big bones, to a hotel the government had taken over right on the water. It wasn't a bonefish camp or lodge, so we had to find our own guide, and we did.

I have found some great guides over the years usually while chugging Bahama Mama's or cold rum and it was no different this night.

A fellow named Jolly Boy came looking as he heard we were looking for a boat and a boat we found. He had a hand painted blue-ishhhh skiff, scow, rowboat; not sure what you'd call it but it had an old Evinrude hitting on three cylinders, so we were golden.

As the night went on, he told us about this huge buoy offshore with all kinds of green fish around it but he hadn't been able to catch any yet.

My buddy and I looked at each other with wheels turning and came up with a plan. I always took a couple of boat rods and tackle on trips for occasions just like this. I had some sea witches and we netted some ballyhoo on the way out.

It was a tight fit with 300- pound Jolly Boy in the back and us two couples filling the two seats but we were rolling. Eight miles out to the tongue of the ocean there was the buoy from hell, it was big as a house and it was full, full, I mean full of life.

You could see the mahi down deep in the moonshine clear water.

I rigged two rods while letting the line out and told Jolly Boy to go faster, faster, faster! He said, "any faster and the bait will be out the watau mon!"

Bam! A dolphin attacked the close line and he was peeling line, "Slow down," I shouted in my over excited voice.' he mumbled something like make my mind up but I was busy, too busy to argue. I got a wrap and pulled the big bull in, beating him to death with a piece of white oak I found in the boat. I think my weasel attitude scared him a bit but we continued to fill the boat with them under the seats, in the bilge, on the girls laps, Blood everywhere, no ice in sight--- yeah, they did things different in the Bahamas.

As the next morning turned to day I had no idea that I would catch what would turn out to be the biggest bonefish of my life to this day.

Jolly Boy showed up with a kalik in his hand saying, " Ya ready, mon?" The three of us today are doing what we came to do because I was a fly fisherman.

We caught some nice bones in the five-pound range and were pretty happy. It was almost time to call it when he noticed bubba.

Jolly Boy started jabbering all kinds of Cajun, Creole, African shit and pointed to this monster of a bone just holding in the current of a trickle. Just laid up.

My skinny legs got to shaking and I made my cast. A blind hog finds an acorn once in a while, they say as my fly landed right in front of him.

I don't know if you ever heard the drag on an Islander fly reel, but it didn't click like normal, it was more like a steady A10 Gatling gun going off, just a loud continuous brrrrrrrrrrrrrr.

The bone and I traded 200 feet of line and backing like it was baseball cards at a kid function.

Back and forth with that steady brrrrrrrr going on and Jolly Boy still talkin Island jabber. The time came and he dug out a net and handed it to my buddy. He said "Hell no, what if I lose it"! Jolly boy replied "I'm not netting it after I saw him yesterday, crazy mon." So, my buddy scooped the now-exhausted fish up and laid it on the deck,

When you come fish with me, I'll tell you how big it was and the rest of the story.

My addiction for bonefish went on like that for many years playing out all across the Caribbean.

Bonefish hippie I was, a Bonefish hippie.

When one thinks of saltwater fish to chase on the long rod, bonefish come to mind.

For the longest time Captain Denny thought God had put them on earth just for the fly fishermen and that is still true but as you will see in the following chapter, redfish now give Mr. bone a run for his money in his opinion.

Bonefish are skittish critters having to feed and live in a shallow environment where everything wants to taste that succulent meat.

It wasn't long ago that the Bahamian government got smart and protected them from commercial harvest.

They had to look above for the birds of prey, horizontally for gill nets and from below where the sharks laid in wait. Hell, I'd be skittish too.

Unlike redfish that sometimes run to your weighted fly for a meal, when bones hear something they make like a twig and split!

Long leaders of 10 to 12 feet and light flies are the norm.

Crazy Charlies, Gotcha's and the Bonefish Bunny to name a few. Just hearing those names again makes him want to wonder, wonder around the Bahamas just being a hippie.

Low Country Tales

10

Before redfish got thick as thieves here in Virginia I had to travel south a bit and I wanted one bad.

A town on the South and North Carolina border fit that bill and plans were made. There was a fly shop on Bay street and the guide I hired out of there was a character indeed.

Rick came with a cigar and a lot of stories about the town and its association with Hollywood.

Seems that a few movie scenes were shot there or in the surrounding area and the stars found the town charming.

The stories came to me second hand and I can't confirm the accuracy, but I'd hate to call him a liar.

One-time Rick was working in the shop when a well-known actor came in, laying some flies on the counter to purchase. When celebrities are out of the spotlight a lot of them don't look like they do in films and this was no exception. When the star handed his credit card to him, Rick looked up after reading it and said, "Oh hell, I didn't recognize you Mr. Jones. Smiling, Tommy said, "hell, I didn't recognize you either. Well it was funny at the time.

The owner of the largest news channel in that era was a regular on the bow of Rick's skiff and at 10 A.M. he was drinking Jack and Coke from a canteen he'd brought. Rick asked if he was going to be ok starting that early, the client replied, "don't worry, I brought two." Laugh out loud.

One day he was in the backyard waiting for a client when his wife came out and told him that Forest Gump was in the front yard, and he was.

A pretty actor that had shaved her head for the lead part in G.I. Jane would frequent the local watering hole while filming there and once danced to her jukebox song with my man. Rick said "he 'ain't been right since".

Enough of stories and hearsay, back to my redfish.

I wanted one bad after seeing them on TV tailing in the grass and fishermen catching them in what looked like their lawn after a good rain.

We met under a bridge that was just featured in a big murder case on TV not long ago. One of the poor kids that hit this bridge in a boat died that night before the driver was murdered a short time after, yeah this town had a lot of stories. You're probably hoping I'll get to the one about my redfish.

We launched mid-morning sight fishing without success the first day but like canteens of whiskey I had two.

The second day while going down a bank the plan was for Rick to pole me while I cast to the grass.

My saltwater rookie ass would false cast several more times than ideal apparently and he came off that platform like a squirrel "I've had enough he barked; you're going to learn to double haul today!"

He pulled over in a quiet cove and for the next hour we practiced while my last chance to catch Mr. Red slipped away, I thought.

It was well worth it and that is the day I got it, the haul and the red.

The tide was dead low as we came upon some hills of oysters higher than the grocery shelf.

Rick said, "There they are, right on the other side of those shells" not seeing them but casting that way, I began to strip and all hell broke loose. The red erupted in the shallow water and hauled ass around the hills and out to the open water. We couldn't go any further because even small skiffs need some water.

I had bought some white rubber boots at a local store the previous day and remember as I jumped overboard in pursuit, him saying, "you're gonna slice up them purdy boots!" Chewing on that cigar and standing up on that perch like he was a raptor.

I chased that fish through the obstacle course until we met in person and by that time, we were a hundred yards from my mentor.

I sloshed back to get a photo of my catch, noticing that my feet were wet and bloody, but it didn't matter, I was now a double haulin, Red fishin, fly fisherman.

The journey as one buddy always tells the author, the journey is the real reason we do this, and he is so right.

People, like characters in a story, are what makes the trips. The dock worker, store attendant and fishing guides. They are the fodder that makes up the meal.

They all have their own personality and that is what makes the story worth telling. You know who they are as you sit and read this.

You can relate by stopping, thinking back to a few that made your day and smile.

As Forrest Gump said "well, that's all I got to say about that."

Sails and a Skort

11

Watching Walker's Cay Chronicles and Spanish Fly took me further south to Costa Rica in search of sailfish on the fly.

Crocodile Bay lodge seemed like a good place to start so we booked, packed and took off in the big bird.

We had three days of fishing planned on one of the 22-foot center consoles with the first day being

"Hell, let's just catch a sailfish day" so we trolled a teaser to bring them up to the surface and threw bait on a spinning rod.

My wife, Tee, had the first chance and did a great job catching a monster on 20-pound test. The sail did put on a show dancing on top more than not and she was happy.

I just had to do it so I flipped a bally to the next one that showed and sealed the deal. That was all fun and games but since I was a fly fisherman the next day was going to be on "Fly Me".

The lodge manager asked if we wanted to upgrade to the flybridge 32 for free and we said "duuuuuuuh" happily agreeing.

The morning dawned calm and humid and with my wife and 12 weight by my side we boarded.

Our captain Cheka barked orders like a fox squirrel and we didn't hit it off on all four cylinders, but we raised sails.

The boat would go out of gear and Cringey, our mate would jerk the teaser out of the water when my quarry was thirty feet or so from the stern. I was to at the same time fling this half a wet chicken out to where the teaser had been.

Cheka like death from above would bark orders: "Cast, cast, cast now!, your other left!, Strip!, Not too fast!, Don't move the fly!"

I had about had it with being bossed around like a child and was thinking to myself how I would like to climb up there and put this gaff to good use, but.....

Well, this went on for a few fish and one thing or another would prevent me from hooking one good.

"Sails, sails!" Cheka barked and there were three, lit up like a cheap diner right behind the boat, Cringey pulled the teaser out just as my fly hit the water and a hole in the Pacific was made. That sail engulfed my super chicken and was off to the bank, greyhounding to the port (looking back that is).

From the captain's lounge we heard "give her a rod, Cast, Cast!" and my nervous wifey did, with a textbook hooking of a sail, textbook.

My sail was still screaming to the left while my wife's fish went to the right and we had a thing, a problem, a real problem.

Both light tackle reels, one spin and one fly were in real danger of being spooled so Captain sabotage, looking down at his new best friend and a 110 pound blonde in a skort and had to make a decision.

Never mind that the purpose of this trip was for me to catch a sail on a fly with me being a fly fisherman and all, but, noooooooooo.

I watched as my bright yellow backing, miles of it, spun off like a reverse cotton candy machine, just never mind that.

As we backed hard port and ole skorty gained line they soon pulled her sail up on the gunnel for a picture.

I tried to be happy for her as I wound 2000 yards of empty line and backing back on my steaming hot reel. I tried my damndest to be happy for her.

While we were there, we met a young Irish charter captain from Martha's Vineyard and his wife, good folks to hang with.

Conor was there to catch a sail on the fly too, We sat at the pool bar stools that night trading similar stories as he didn't connect that day either.

They were to fish with our Capt. Cheka the next morning so I wished them luck and we retired for the night.

We drew a smaller center console with an American captain the next day and chose to still pursue sails instead of going for roosterfish like planned, because I was a skunked fly fisherman.

My wife boarded first in her baggy khaki fishing pants I'd suggested for the outing and then I boarded with my rod and wet chicken.

The captain seemed nice and the drill was the same for the day and it didn't take long for him to scream 'Marlieeen, marlieeen!" Grabbing my rod from the bucket and looking back all I saw was white water as the three hundred pound class blue marlin was destroying his teaser. They were in a tug of war with it wrapped around his bill but Cap prevailed and I cast.

Not unlike other memories I have shared with you, this one has its place etched in my brain.

My skinny knees got to shaking again as I stripped the fly with the Marlin slashing at it, boat out of gear, slick calm-- just imagine all this only 20 feet from the boat. Take a second and imagine.

Me overthinking the situation like a dog chasing a car: "What the hell am I going to do with it if he does eat my fly?"

Well, he didn't and looking down at my ten fingers maybe it was a good thing he didn't.

Conor's fly stuck that day with proof being a photograph taken of him with my sail and his rod in his teeth.

A fly rod because he was a Fly Fisherman.

Captain Denny still has yet to get that sailfish on a fly, but one needs a goal in life. At 68 years of age and starting a new guide business evidently it isn't over just yet.

Traveling has gotten a lot harder since 9/11 for sure. That was a long time ago. Before that you could just get on a big bird with a cigarette and real glass of wine, metal silverware and carry your fishhooks and knives up front with you, a long time ago.

The day may come when a group asks, or his kids insist on a big trip and they go south for a visit.

I hear the hook has rusted out of his Sail's mouth and he is bigger, meaner and wiser.

Now that's what I call a goal!

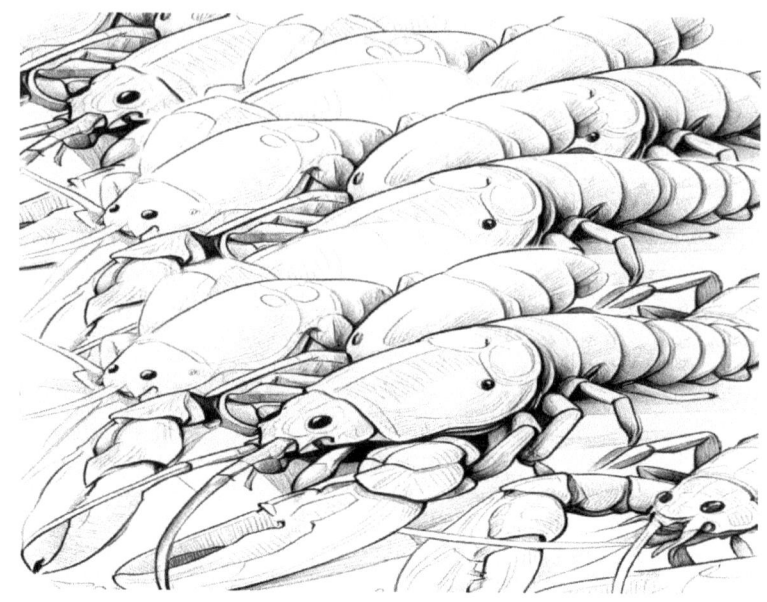

Bass & Lobsta
12

We were invited up to Martha's Vineyard to catch massive striped bass or rockfish as we call them in the Chesapeake by Conor and his wife so we showed up in May when the time got right.

The first night there, Conor went to get dinner and came back with Maine Lobsters and I was looking forward to that. It was a rare and expensive night out if we went and had lobstah back in the Shenandoah Valley.

I expected a lobster each but what we got was more like a blue crab feed on the bay. He mounded up a pile of bugs like they call them in the Bahamas.

Not complaining we dug in and ate lobstas until we were full like ticks. What a treat.

The morning dawned foggy and calm as he and I boarded his Mako 28 for the white- knuckled ride around the island in the fog. The Irish are just built different.

Arriving at x marks the spot there wasn't much going on, slick calm, dead tide and no birds, nothing.

"When the tide starts, we'll get em" he said. It almost sounded like "you should have been here yesterday" but then it happened. I really thought it was a tsunami or something getting ready to start. The sea just rose up in an angry line of four footers with us just a cast away in mill pond conditions.

Damndest thing I'd ever seen. "There," Conor pointed to the wall of water and you could see in it, like looking into an aquarium. Bright red squid being chased by three-foot striped bass "Get it out there Man!" Why has everybody got to holler? I thought to myself.

I made some back casts avoiding the tee top and dropped my red fly on the rip. Damn I love it when a plan comes together.

I have a picture on my study wall of me and this 38" bass with a rod draped over my arm. A fly rod, it was a good time.

We meet good people on the water, for the most part they will do anything for you if you are just you. Don't put up a front or think you are a better fisherman or person for that matter.

Those are words to live by, the author thinks as it has worked for him for almost 7 decades. That's a lot of experience day in and day out.

If you treat people the way you want to be treated you will find opportunities exist well beyond your financial means.

He has been on trips with people way out of his pay scale, people that took a liking to him for his blunt honesty. Something that is almost unheard of today but if you are yourself in this world of spam and fake news, you will go far pilgrim.

Southbound

13

We had enough of the harsh long winters in the Shenandoah Valley so decided to move to Florida.

Upon settling in and still running my ole Go-Devil to skirt the rocks in the Nature Coast area we got to know the backcountry pretty well.

I had traveled the area, enough to know by now what boat I needed to build--a tank!

I ended up with a 20' SeaArk with a half tower for better visibility. As far as fly fishing goes, when one thinks of Florida, they think of tarpon but the real fishery lies in redfish, trout and snook.

I myself would rather put folks on more opportunities than one angler taking half the day fighting a fish. After all, the real thrill in fly fishing is the cast, presentation and hook up, not the fight.

In the following chapters I will take you on a trip down memory lane in Yankeetown Florida, a town built long ago where the Withlacoochee River meets the Gulf.

The town was started as an angling town for northerners to escape the cold winters, as we did.

The waters are fertile and clear with the winters going below freezing on occasion in the winter.

When the cold comes, so does great fishing and the following pages will give you a taste of running the backcountry on the Nature Coast.

Most northern fly fishermen and women long for the feel of the UV rays down south.

Be careful what you wish for. The heat in the sunshine state can get almost unbearable 4 months out of the year.

If you have a bigger boat and are able to fish near and offshore it isn't too bad, but for backcountry junkies like the author it's a 6 month at most kind of activity and then you better get it done early or late in the day.

The younger folk can handle the heat a lot better and the sun is different than when the Capt' roamed the flats close to the equator.

The move will never be thought of as a bad thing because there were some very good times and some very good friends were made.

Life goes on.

Negative One

14

As the hot summers faded to a comfy temperature in October the low tides would go negative on the new and full moons.

The fish in the backcountry would congregate in smaller areas and the elevation change, though slight, would create a current like a stream in some places and we all know fish love moving water, all fish.

"The Beast" had a jet outboard that allowed us to get to places away from the crowd but there were dangers. The area was nothing but limestone rock at low tide, brutal on equipment thus the name "lower unit graveyard of the Gulf", but it was great for wading which in turn was good for a fly fisherman and after all I was a fly fisherman.

I'd cruise in just inches of water to my landing area that was a hole deeper than the surrounding area, chop the power and settle in.

We then would wade to the areas that held fish. It was great for the wife and I as she could take her spinning rod and I my whip in the opposite direction.

You had to mind the tide, or you could get trapped by water too deep for your waders when the tide returned.

Some holes were as small as a house and on certain days would be full of reds, trout and snook resulting in hooking up on every cast. Other days the same hole would be void of life. The trick was learning where to start and work your way with the incoming tide, so each destination was as good as the last, yep, that was the trick and it took years to learn.

A favorite tactic of mine was at dead low tide I would blast back in the creeks passing schools of mullet and redfish moving in with the tide until I got to my favorite ambush spot well past the fish.

I then would get out, walk to a sandbar and wait.

It was more like fishing in Alaska than the tropics dressed in warm waders and beanies. It sure didn't look like the Florida most envision for shur.

The mullet and baitfish would be the first to appear flipping and boiling, then shortly after you would see the reds, hungry and ready to fight.

A crab or baitfish pattern would get attention and the fishing would be off the chain.

Then like snow in March they would be gone, passing you to wherever they had their minds set on.

In the longer creeks you could play hopscotch a time or two repeating the process.

Winter was great for that reason along with the lack of snakes, bugs, brutal heat and alligators.

I met a fellow with a reputation bigger than Texas, lets just call him Bill. He was and is the best tarpon guide in the area and had some experience with the winter backcountry fishing.

We hit it off pretty good with his knowledge of the fish, tactics and area and my 25 years' experience with shallow running machines. We were a production team, a fish producing team that is.

We scouted and learned the area right back to the tree line finding fish in nooks and crannies you wouldn't believe. It was good.

As time went on my passion for fly fishing lured me into solitude, we only passed each other on occasion, me in "the Beast" and he in his brand new and improved Go-Devil. We would stop, trade spots like cards, tell stories and be on our way. Bill is a true living legend to this day.

My best snook I ever caught on the fly was a 37" beast of a fighter. In the current between oyster bars in March.

It was in an area that on a negative would create current that would knock you off your feet. Snook love moving water.

I beached the "Beast" on an oyster bar that has been there since the birth of Jesus. Got out like I had just stepped off the floats of a seaplane in the north country and proceeded to the water on the opposite side.

The first cast of the white deceiver was inhaled by a bucket mouth bitch, immediately went airborne shaking that head with leader slicing gill plates flaring, what a sight in my memory bank.

She stayed in the air until she didn't, then she sounded with that massive tail propelling her across the creek which made me happy, the less time spent in the air slashing those gills the better.

After a long fight she decided to come to papa, and I pulled her on the bar and carefully took the fly from her.

What a beautiful fish with that black stripe, yellow/green tail and coal black eyes staring into her capturer's eyes. 'Magine.

I held her in the water with her sucking my thumb like a small child waiting for the muscles to relax and breathing to return knowing full well we would never meet again.

She slowly let go and shoved off like it was just a dream for the both of us.

The backcountry was magical.

Wading the backcountry was the most fun to be had for a man with a jet or airboat on the nature coast.

Not unlike the ESVA the place is a wilderness. You could run all day and not see a boat. It changed a lot in the 6 years the author was there.

Mud boats caught on fast as a cheap way to get from point A to point B. You could expect to see a few boats in the back during the last couple years.

That's a double edge sword as when there is no one around with the kind of boat it takes to access the area, it can be not only inconvenient but dangerous.

There were more than a few times when the Captain' would hear a call for help and get up from the lazy chair, launch "The Beast" and go on a rescue.

Fishing back there was not for the weak of heart as hard limestone rocks would stick up just below the surface to end the lower unit on a normal boat. There were many field repairs on the boat hulls to get back to the dock, but the fishing was legendary.

There were names of fishing locations that only a few with big gonads knew like Hell's Gate, Jurassic Park, The ledge and Hole in the wall.

It's a wild place for sure and if you have the desire to fish truly wilderness areas the author knows a few fly guides down there so get up with him for some recommendations.

Jacks or Better

15

While in Florida I met a new fish, a fish that if human would be named Rodney because he gets no respect, at least until you catch one.

I'm sure you have heard and seen the videos of G.T.s eating birds in the Indian Ocean and pursued by anglers in the upper tax bracket. I think I would have to get a second mortgage to hunt them.

Anyway, they are in the Jack family, a fish that someone must have pissed in their cereal because they had an attitude while still in the egg.

Of all the fish that swim in the salt including bonefish, Jack Crevalle fight like no other. They have a huge forked tail for speed but also a flat wide body, imagine a 20 pound bluegill, and you get the picture.

One morning the tide was even too low for "The Beast" to enter the creeks and my brother, Gary and I were staging outside in the gulf waiting and chewing the fat.

There was a deep canal that fed the old power plant off to the south and out of it as the tide flooded they came. Schools of sickle tails sticking out of the water like permit and heading straight for us.

I grabbed my 9 weight with the Islander reel and waited on the bow, we were aground in about 6" of water so fate would have to bring them into range, and it did.

These skinny legs though much older began to shake while my brother stood in the water leaning on the stern.

I cast to the lead fish and "Holy shit" this fish was about to teach me all about respect. He was a quarter mile from deep water and bound and determined to get to it. That steady Brrrrrrrr sound came from my reel but there was no trading line with this guy, he just ran and ran.

I screwed the drag knob down as it got closer to the end of my backing in desperation hoping my leader held and it did.

He ran until he just couldn't run anymore. I envisioned the scene from Forrest Gump playing out underwater when he was running and his braces came off in pieces, well, that's what I envisioned.

I began the long retrieve of my line while I heard my brother yell "fish on" behind me still in the water.

His movie was not unlike mine as Rodney disappeared around the mangroves.

Releasing mine we cranked up the now freed boat and gave chase.

Pictures were taken, fists were bumped, and a new favorite fish became.

With respect.

If you watch "You Tube" enough about fly-fishing in the salt, a show about the monster giant trevally will probably show up.

The journey to catch one can be expensive and time consuming. Some folks don't have either but there is an alternative and that is to fish for jack crevalle or AKA canal tuna.

They are common in Florida and other southern states and on an 8 or 9 wt. fly rod are a true challenge.

When hungry they take a top water fly with gusto, fight like a champ and are easy to get to.

Next time you're down south look 'em up and give them respect because they deserve it.

<u>Airboat Diaries</u>
<u>16</u>

I just had to have it, my need to get to the shallowest places coerced me into taking the plunge.

I'd seen them running by me on top of the mud while I sat eating Vienna sausages aground waiting on the tide.

It was a love hate relationship, me being a fly fisherman loving peace and solitude but wanting to get into the wildest outback possible.

I should have named her "Oxymoron" with a blacked-out cage and fire breathing headers sporting two fly rods hanging off the back like CB antennas from Smokey and the Bandit.

What a sight, but she was hell when she was well and there lies the problem. An airboat driver needs to keep more tools on board than fuel.

Keeping one together in the rocky saltwater environment was totally different from the grassy freshwater area they were intended for.

Good thing I was a fly fisherman because I had no room for bait.

I got stuck more times in that widowmaker than my jet due to overconfidence and lack of power.

There are airboats that can run on dry bare ground and sticky mud but Oxymoron wasn't one of them.

One time my brave wife and I were fishing in a tournament and knew where some good redfish lived.

Jurassic Park, a place we named for the size of the fish that dined there. It was a small creek that during low tide dried up to just wet mud and rocks.

At noon the tide fell below negative 1' and we knew if we could get there it was a done deal. We set out not unlike astronauts when they leave, not knowing if they can return.

We arrived at the perfect time, so shallow the bait wasn't even there yet. I pulled her up on this mud bar so when the tide came in the fish would be able to pass, that's how small an area we are talking about.

Crawling up the bank and going downstream to a bar sticking out of the water where I could cast, we waited.

The mullet were the first, flipping and doing the happy jumps and behind were the hungry reds.

First, when the water was still crazy low the smaller fish arrived but as the water rose the big uns came to the party. Wifey was the first to hook up landing a perfect slot fish, on the board we thought.

Then it was my time to cast losing a beast by the oysters cutting my leader.

Patched up and back in the game, yes! Another perfect upper slot fish. Wham bam thank ya mam and we were done.

One problem, it was one of those rare days when the tide was held out by the wind and she wasn't coming.

Here we are with what we think is the two winning fish sitting on a sticky mud bar in an underpowered airboat with weigh in time approaching.

'Moron was stuck. It was approaching dark and we began to worry beyond the tournament. Spending the night out there in the cold marsh wasn't in the plan.

I called a buddy with a mud boat to come to the rescue, but he couldn't get closer than a mile or so away. I called another airboat captain that I know was out and he said he was on his way.

Somewhere along the way his oil cap came off and spewed all his oil out of the engine and when he got to the mud boat he noticed and had to stop.

Now we have a stuck mud boat with an airboat out of oil, a clusterfuck in the making and I hear no laughing out loud. Matter of fact I hear nothing because they are too far away.

Airboat #1 calls his buddy Airboat #2 for rescue with a case of oil and he came in due time because he had to go beer and oil shopping.

It all came together finally just before dark with weigh in long past.

We all went to the tourney to get some dinner and tell stories about the two winning fish still in the marsh on the boat. It was two days before we had a tide big enough to go retrieve the 'Moron with "The Beast".

Airboat for sale.

If there ever was an oxymoron, a fly fisher in an airboat is the one. An airboat is the most hated vehicle by the peace-loving public consisting of kayakers, fishermen and what not.

To see a noisy airboat with fly rods onboard is not normal by any stretch of imagination.

In the winter the tides get negative and leave miles of mud where the water receded, leaving pools of water teaming with fish. It is a great place to take new fly fishers.

The casts are short, the fish are hungry, and you are wading, so you can get away from all the false casts.

I don't think the 'Moron ever saw another airboat with a fly rod.

Rearview Town

17

I can say I been there, done that, and got the tee-shirt. Our friends in Florida are what we miss the most, but things change, and one must adapt.

My brother, Gary, who came by vehicle quite often got the C word and I don't mean Covid, my love for heat was evaporating and a new world class fishery was developing back in my stomping grounds.

Yes, Virginia was calling me home, so we sold out, shook the sand off, shook hands and threw the dog in the truck.

We were born in the Shenandoah Valley as you know by now, but I spent half my life growing up on the Eastern Shore so wanting to be closer to the salt we built our home by the water in Onancock, Va.

We are less than 5 hrs. from our homeland so my healing brother and one of my sons have a shorter ride to see Pappy.

I took a couple years to re-explore the area I knew so well back in the "Danger Zone" days before opening a guide service.

Shoals had shifted, the water got warmer and we had a lot more fishes hanging out from the south.

The puppy drum as they call them have created a world class destination for fly fishing.

The cobia sight fishing thing shifted from the Gulf states to the Chesapeake Bay and bull drum have invaded the bay and seaside in greater numbers.

Yes, Virginia has become the sport fishing destination overtaking many of the southern states in my opinion.

The following chapters will take a peek into the depths of "The Old Dominion".

There's not much to say about this chapter except, things change and the older you get the faster that happens.

Younger folks should sit a spell and reflect occasionally, pour a mixer, grab a Modelo or hell, smoke a joint.

Reflect on what you have done with your life and fishing.

Don't be in a hurry to catch the biggest fish that swims. Enjoy the little ones that need love too.

Reflecting is good, there was once a guy in our club that would invite the Capt' to dove hunt in Virginia every year and he often said that he liked it better when the birds flew at a more controlled pace. Not all at once. Mike liked to walk out, pick his dove up and return to his stool at a casual pace. Sit and reflect on the shot, the sky and the full monty as they say across the pond.

Mike is gone now as are most of the author's friends that he shared boats and blinds with.

I think that gives him the right to politely ask you to reflect occasionally.

Please do.

<u>Run That Dog</u>
<u>18</u>

Puppy drum as they call them here in VA instead of redfish are thick as 'skeeters on the shore now.

Redfish, as I will refer to them in my opinion, are one of the top fly-fishing critters you can pursue.

They eat a fly like a dog on a bone, pull hard enough to put you on the reel and are accessible to anyone with a small boat or kayak.

On seaside as we call it here is an area more than 800 sq. miles with some of the most beautiful uninhabited marsh in the United States.

There are barrier islands with a rich history of once being occupied though mother nature was the winner in the end forcing all to withdraw.

A vast wetland with at times mosquitoes and green flies big enough to have N numbers.

The redfish now a days stay here in good numbers right through the winter months but April to early December are prime times.

My new guide service "Botangles Fly Fishing" caters to bug slingers no matter the experience level.

I have made enough money in my life to get by in retirement and only do it for the love of it, the love of watching someone fling flies through the air and on rare occasions hitting their mark.

There is nothing like watching a lifelong trout fisherman or a lady from down at the bank new to the sport, hook and land a red for the first time.

"Ok, look to your 1 o'clock two boat lengths away, u see 'em? There's two of 'em?

"Uhhhhhhh","Point your rod....."Oh! I got 'em now!"

I watch from my perch above "The Beast" while they fling that black leggy critter to within a foot and drag it into view of the pair. Usually when one gets a glimpse of it, they race for it with the winner loosing.

I see the gills flare as the red dog inhales it. "Strip hard" I say, and the water explodes! "Yeah!"

Hooking an eight-pound fish in 6" of water results in such an action, along with my first timer yelling in glee and clearing the line from feet, cleats, trolling motor and the reel handle.

If all that went well, the rod goes to 45 degrees to clear oyster beds and the war starts.

Redfish were put on earth for the fly fishermen and we are fly fishermen even though a growing percent are women and we do welcome them with open arms.

I think in the long run women make better anglers, their patience and different way of looking at the picture just makes it so.

My wife Tee, a great angler, is just now starting to use the whip more as I think the redfish are so abundant and easy to catch here, it makes good sport again.

The big Bulls upwards of 30 pounds with some going 50 swim onto the flats in the spring looking for warmer water. This is a new fishery, but old timers knew about it but kept it hush like they did tarpon for years.

Yes, the Eastern Shore is a "land lost in time" as they say and I'm glad to be lost with it.

A land with what I think has the best red fishing on the planet, but one must have the best of equipment, a half 'ah century of knowledge and some huge Gonads to find 'em.

Redfish, redfish and more redfish are what a person on the shore thinks now. Some flounder fishermen have even called them a nuisance.

Reds will always hold a spot in a saltwater fly fisherman's heart as they are the perfect quarry.

Unlike bonefish they are user friendly letting you drop a dumbbell eye'd fly right in front of them without them running for the door.

Nuisance or not they are the new sheriff in town on the ESVA and we should embrace them.

__In Closing__
__19__

The sport of fly fishing has changed like everything else in my lifetime from fashion, equipment, destinations and gender.

50 years ago, there were only a handful of women in the sport, or pastime as I like to think of it. Now women make up the largest growing segment.

As far as fashion, I would have liked to have seen my face if standing in the creek with my old green rubber waders and cargo shirt saw a tinker bell looking fella coming down the bank.

Tights with a skort on top, a silk hooded shirt with a face mask looking like he was going to rob a bank, a backpack having enough equipment and extra rods to spend a week when his electric car is right up on the bank, (LOL).

I have adjusted some, wearing some light hood shirts but can't get used to the masks as I lay here all bandaged up from skin cancer surgery.

I love my Simms waders but draw the line on

Those tights and a skort.

I've tried the new way and ask the younger ones to try, just for one day to leave some at home.

Grab a few flies, an extra leader and tippet and take a walk. It was the simplicity that got me hooked and for old time sakes just try it.

Fly fishermen and women, I have noticed, are like a bodybuilder wanna be. In most garages across America there are two unused items, a set of workout equipment and a cheap fly rod.

Both taking time to use right, and time is from what I understand, hard to come by these days.

I've learned from following up on my fly fishing classes that the rate of folks continuing is low, very low.

Most passionate fly people just pick it up and roll with it, most are self-taught with a YouTube video or online course. They are the type A or B blood brothers and sisters.

"You can lead a horse to water, but you can't make him drink," so if you have achieved success and are out there flinging and smiling, congrats.

I don't care if you wear a smock, you are a blood brother and sister of mine and are welcome on my boat at any time just leave the lipstick at home please.

May God bless whether you drink White Claw, Modelo or Bud, you keep safe, keep it simple and come fish with me. We can laugh at ourselves.

Capt' D

Full circle comes to mind when one thinks about the captain's journey back to his roots, back to the neighborhood where he cut his teeth, with an old bamboo pole found in a closet.

"Half the fun is getting there"

_ _ Captain Bill Nast

www.ingramcontent.com/pod-product-compliance
Lightning Source LLC
Chambersburg PA
CBHW061700120626
46550CB00003B/1027